REPARATIONS NOW!

REPARATIONS NOW!

POEMS *by* ASHLEY M. JONES

HUB CITY PRESS
SPARTANBURG, SC

Design Lead: Meg Reid
Editor: Katherine Webb
Cover Painting: © Erin LeAnn Mitchell

Library of Congress
Cataloging-in-Publication Data

Names: Jones, Ashley M., 1990 - author.
Title: Reparations now! : poems / by Ashley M Jones.
Description: Spartanburg, SC : Hub City Press, [2021]
Identifiers:
    LCCN 2021006386
    ISBN 9781938235863 (paperback)
    ISBN 9781938235870 (ebook)
Subjects: LCGFT: Poetry.
Classification:
    LCC PS3610.O595 R47 202
    DDC 811/.6—dc23
LC record available at https://lccn.loc.gov/2021006386

"Friendly Skies, or, Black Woman Speaks Herself Into God"; "Superman's Girlfriend Lois Lane No. 106";
"Soul Power/James Brown Time Loop" appeared in *The Future of Black: An Afrofuturism & Black Comics
Poetry Anthology.*
"I Cannot Talk About The South Without Talking About Black Women" appeared previously in *Southern
Women.*
"Photosynthesis"; "All Y'all Really From Alabama"; "Love Note: Surely"; "Contrapuntal with Gladys
Knight and Infidelity" appeared previously in *Ice on a Hot Stove: Poetry From the Converse Low Residency MFA*

Hub City Press gratefully acknowledges support from the National Endowment for the Arts,
the Amazon Literary Partnership, South Arts, and the South Carolina Arts Commission.

Manufactured in the United States of America
First Edition

HUB CITY PRESS
186 W. Main Street
Spartanburg, SC 29306
864.577.9349 | www.hubcity.org

for Dad, who taught me how to love and how to fight
for Armand, whose laughter was light

Table Of Contents

For Donald Lewis Jones

Dad, every blade of grass wears your name,
on the wind, you laugh in great swaths of air.
Now, the days feel more like years because you're gone,
only memories hold your voice
and the crack of your knees stretching in the night.

Listen, I want to tell you about a man who was deliberate,
delicate in his loving. Complete in his care.
Let me show you my skin, my blood which is his.
Even the sunrise I hold with his eyes,
which are my eyes. My heart which is his.

In the quiet times, we wonder where you are.
Sometimes, feels like your truck will turn the corner
just in time for dinner. Your keys chiming up the stairs.
Out in the garden, your plants still grow.
Now, we will give them water and time,
every season, a harvest started by your hands,
showing your love, all-encompassing, forever.

Hymn Of Our Jesus & The Holy Tow Truck

after Mary Szbist

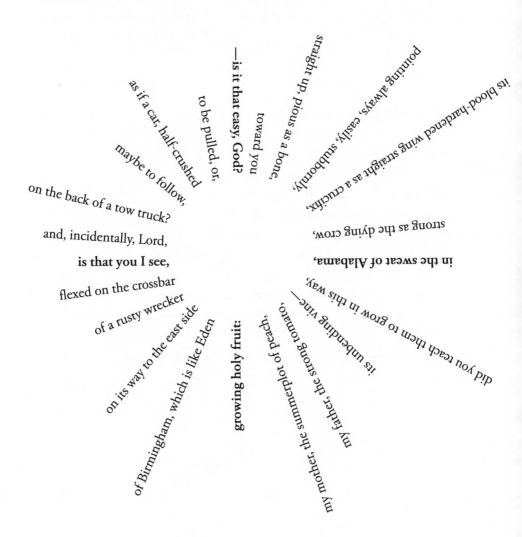

—is it that easy, God?

to be pulled, or,

as if a car, half-crushed

maybe to follow,

on the back of a tow truck?

and, incidentally, Lord,

is that you I see,

flexed on the crossbar

of a rusty wrecker

on its way to the east side

of Birmingham, which is like Eden

growing holy fruit:

my mother, the summerplot of peach,

my father, the strong tomato,

its unbending vine,

did you teach them to grow in this way,

in the sweat of Alabama,

strong as the dying crow,

its blood-hardened wing straight as a crucifix,

pointing always, easily, stubbornly,

straight up, pious as a bone,

toward you

Mary, Don't You Weep, Or, Mary Turner Resurrected

When Mary Turner threatened to press charges for the wrongful lynching of her husband in Brooks County, Georgia on May 19, 1918, she was strung upside down, her clothes were burned off, and her unborn baby was cut from her womb and stomped to death. Turner was shot repeatedly, and she and her baby were buried close by their murder site.

like all resurrections, it began with blood, dirt,
                    unending light—
the georgia moss punctuated by camellias, their white hurt
stretching across brooks county—no blight
to stain their leaves, just the ash falling, bloody
from mary's emblazoned womb. her baby, a fire,
its single soft cry still igniting the air—could it be
that even this baby, even this one-breathed-angel was crucified
to save us all? maybe.
                    maybe mary and her baby flew up from death
                    in sweaty georgia—her shallow grave shaken loose. finally free,
                    resurrected—it turns out, all along hell was earth,
what else could she name that rock covered in leaf and loam,
not loving, not hopeful, and most certainly not home.

Stephon Don't You Moan, Or, To Serve And Protect

22 year-old father of two, Stephon Clark, was shot twenty times on March 19, 2018, by Sacra-
mento Police in his grandmother's backyard. The gun police claim to have seen him carrying
was his iPhone.

is there a police protocol for grace,
for the moment between *show us your hands* and shoot? that night,
policeman, servant of the gun, did you give   space

for a man's innocence to bloom? despite
                              the loaded weight of your finger on the trigger,
              despite   how the night
              painted that man bigger,
made him a giant with a fireball in his hands? despite the loud explosion of your fright?
innocence is for softer things—an open, empty palm, a blooming flower,
                                        a spread of rocks becoming sand.
silly civilization, you thought we'd evolved beyond *abuse of power,*
but again, a pruning. what a flower you were, stephon—and
what holiness in your body opening, petaled in the white helicopter light—
this, an armageddon of bullets, flowers, stars, stripes.

The Kid Next To Me At The 7pm Showing Of The Avengers Has A Toy Gun

: and is wearing black flip flops
: has commented, loudly, for the entire feature presentation
: is pointing it at his mom
: is clicking the plastic hinges on its expanding arm—
    fist for a bullet—so it sounds like scissors
: is still salty around the lips from his movie popcorn
: will later regret this tub of movie popcorn, intestine-bound
: is pulling the trigger over and over and maybe once in my direction
: is shooting up this whole theater to the tune of this dramatic and
    opulent theme song
: is restless, but what else will boys be
: chatters about sequels, every word a click click triggerpull triggerpull
: is, incidentally, about the size of Tamir Rice
: is alive and will keep living
—and wait
       do I need to tell you the color of his skin?

In My Dream, I'm Shot Again And Again

only, in this world, I'm not me. or, I'm me and not me simultaneously—my dream-self is split. the me part watches the other me—a man I knew when we were both children here in reality; a man I knew to have trouble walking—we didn't focus on the medical specifics back then—my school was such that it erased those arbitrary boundaries; I knew this boy as charismatic and kind; I saw this boy a few months back—a man now, as time had chipped away the fat in our cheeks and the white in our eyes—and his spirit was the same, so full of a tender love I always wished I could crawl into; the kind of man who looks at his mother with a softness of a man who loves his mother. in my dream, I am myself and this man, simultaneously. the neighborhood, quiet as a dream, spread out green and tide grey before us. then, the spark: a man walks up—does he bump into me? into the other me? a man walks up and he's angry—we can see the way his lips stretch against his teeth, the way his rage foams up in little puddles at the corners of his mouth. I'm yelling and I'm yelling at myself to stop yelling, and then I try to run but my legs, they've never been so quick, and never quicker than the bullets I feel, sharp blades of light in my back, over and over, the blood metallic and pooling, my breaths interrupted by each new bullet lodging itself into my body. I watch myself writhe in never-death—they say you can't die in a dream, but I'm wishing for it, I'm looking at myself be killed but never dead, I'm begging myself to *just wake up*, the man's hand pinkening against his gun, then his eyes look up at me, the me that isn't on the ground, and then it's my turn, and then it's both of us on the ground, and it's so green, and the pain, it's singing now, and maybe if I just lean *in in in* the pain will feel like a song—

Soul Power / James Brown Time Loop

everything is color and sweat, like the
pinwheel that marks a time jump on *justice
league* or *wonder twins* or *batman & robin.*
it's all spinning to the tune of those horns
in "soul power" by james brown, who was,
i think, some kind of superman, because
he wore a cape / because he could see
through you to the whitemeat / because
his heart was wrapped in a blanket of green
glowing money, faster than a speeding
bullet, funkier than george clinton stewing
in a vat of radioactive gym socks, he was
the originator of a time loop, of a horns
section that would not (could not) quit,
of a bridge that led nowhere but from one
side of his growling throat to the dark loud
other, and it's here, in this time loop, in
this trumpeted commercial break, that i
see just how caught up i really am—

—the man i did not love is sitting at my dining room table, gobbling up a cake i
baked for his unremarkable birthday, and in the spitshine of his teeth, emerges the
metal-shining smile of the other man i did not love, who did not love me, gobbling
up the edits i made, painstakingly, on his poems, and in the ink, black and boogey-
ing on the page, rose the whiskers of the other man i did not love, framing his slow
and drawling mouth, his words slipping, thick, out of his lips, and then they were
all the same man, in an endless, spinning, trumpet-filled infinity in which, yes, i
could get on down down down down down, but not out. every wall a new man
dancing a two step to a tune that will end in my demise—

—and james is telling me how i got ta got ta feel it, and maybe he's right. this is the funkiest hurt but it got to hurt, it got to, james said so, cause when it's finally over, when the trumpets quiet down, my body still knows how to dance all over the beat still pounding in my heart, how to recognize these unrelenting sounds, these men making dissonant music, how to turn that hard hurt beat into my own sure feet stomping it into beauty.

negative cycle in relationships
↳ men she doesn't love
gobbling up the effort
she gives

time loop ↴
repetitive

9

The Horns, According To James Brown

get back
> cause I hit back
>> with my hand
>> or my band—

don't matter
> if

you master
> or servant
>> my little baby
>> or my old lady

I don't miss.

this funk
> goesssssssssss and goooooooooes—

> war, peace, chicken grease—

I'm proud/LOUD

and you better believe
> my money is black
>> as my ass
>> and just as hard
>> to catch.

What Lives In The If in Al Green's "Simply Beautiful"

in the room of my love
there is a whole
world—

      there is a bass guitar that plays all by itself.
      there is fire in the hearth, crackling
      and there is a brown hue all over—that's my skin.
      my skin and my love are inseparable.

in the room of my love
there is a growl and a giggle,
there is a never-ending meal—

      cornbread and collard greens and hamhocks and neckbones and sweet potato
      pie and mac and cheese (the good kind not the kind at church or the kind
      that one aunt swears is good or the kind in a blue box) and potatosalad/
      barbecueribs/coleslaw/bakedbeans/cornonthecob/poundcake all on the same
      plate and grape Kool Aid and spring water and broccoli&cheese casserole and
      fried chicken and smothered pork chops and sausage&gravy and pancakes
      and butter and—

in the room of my love there is room, maybe for you,
but only if Al Green is playing and only if your hand is shaped, love,
                          like a key—

Home Security

Two thousand three hundred miles away from home
and I'm watching the tiny camera attached to the back of my parents' house.

Brother dragging the black trash bin to the curb, sister's hum
to the backdoor with her key and bag in hand. The breaths of our quiet house.

I've been thinking, lately, about time, how it will come
for me and my family, will steal these bones, the flesh that guards like a house.

I've been thinking about getting older, the way it seems like some
years pass quick as a snap, my life between two fingers. My body an aging house—

the cracks and creaks down the halls. How did I become
so old that I can start to see the end of this horizon, my mind a house

full of impending pain? Imminent pain. My father's face a tomb
of tears at his mother's grave. My mother's sighs through the Greensboro house

now emptied of my grandmother's body. The way a headstone smiles, *come
now, did you think you'd really live forever?* On the home security camera, my house

looks indestructible. The cars unmoving, as if everyone has come
home to stay. Looking at them walk in and out of the house,

my parents and my siblings look something like strangers. How the camera's numb
eye can't capture memory, just pixels and pigments—it can't keep my house

from becoming a pile of wood and shingled crumb—
can't keep those living in it from dissolving into darkness, dirt, the big house

I imagine as heaven. Maybe, then, my angel-parents wave me home
from their golden porch. They say: *Ashley, we've been waiting—come on in the house.*

Meteor Shower

There is nothing particularly funny about rocks flying through the sky, the raccoon gobbling trash next door, the empty street, but we laugh like it's Christmas, or like those rare summer mornings on the back porch when the sun isn't too hot and everything is possible. There's a meteor shower tonight, and we feel large and happy standing in our driveway. We strain our eyes for something lit up, carrying wishes or a bonfire of dreams ready to alight from the sky. Maybe, like the man they say rides the night this time of year, we will see something impossible, impossibly generous. It's a blessing to receive a gift—to get something hoped for, something named and exhaled on a piece of space sediment. To get a half hour sitting here, next to these loves of mine, to feel the easy way my laugh twinkles out until I'm all sky, mouth open like this whole world is a big bright drink. We don't see the meteors falling in a trail of smoke. We wait almost an hour for their shine across the sky. And although we don't see anything but these domesticated stars, there is something singular—maybe the way my sister's eyes hold the starglow, my brother's humming speech, my dad standing here, healthy and smiling among his four children—once in a lifetime, these meteors, this night.

Photosynthesis

When I was young, my father taught us
how dirt made way for food,
how to turn over soil so it would hold a seed,
an infant bud, how the dark could nurse it
until it broke its green arms out to touch the sun.
In every backyard we've ever had, he made a little garden plot
with room for heirloom tomatoes, corn, carrots,
peppers: jalapeño, bell, and poblano—
okra, eggplant, lemons, collards, broccoli, pole beans,
watermelon, squash, trees filled with fruit and nuts,
brussels sprouts, herbs: basil, mint, parsley, rosemary—
onions, sweet potatoes, cucumber, cantaloupe, cabbage,
oranges, swiss chard and peaches,
sunflowers tall and straightbacked as soldiers,
lantana, amaryllis, echinacea,
pansies and roses and bushes bubbling with hydrangeas.
Every plant with its purpose,
flowers to bring worms and wasps. How their work matters here.

This is the work we have always known,
pulling food and flowers from a pile of earth.
The difference, now: my father is not a slave,
not a sharecropper. This land is his and so is this garden,
so is this work. The difference is that he owns this labor.
The work of his own hands for his own belly,
for his own children's bellies. We eat because he works.

This is the legacy of his grandmother, my great-granny—
Ollie Mae Harris and her untouchable flower garden.

Just like her hats, her flowerbeds sprouted something special,
plants and colors the neighbors could only dream of.
He was young when he learned that this beauty is built on work—
the cows and the factories in their stomachs,
the fertilizer they spewed out—
the stink that brought such fragrance. What you call waste,
I call power. What you call work I make beautiful again.

In his garden, even problems become energy, beauty—
my father has ended many work days in the backyard,
worries of the firehouse dropping like grain, my father wrist-deep
in soil. I am convinced the earth speaks back to him
as he feeds it—it is a conversational labor, gardening.
The seeds tell him what they will be, the soil tells seeds how to grow,
my father speaks sun and water into the earth,
we hear him, each harvest, his heartbeat sweet, like fruit.

She Is Beauty, She Is Grace

for Breonna Taylor and Sandra Bland and Oluwatoyin Salau and so many killed B

My mother always told me I was beautiful.
She oiled my scalp with proud-mother care.
She bought me baby and Barbie dolls
who shared my skin—brown beauties
who smiled back at me, whose infinite stories
I told each day in my playtime heaven.
My mother gave me dreams and a Barbie Dreamhouse.
She gave me the right way to tie my shoes
and tuck my shirt. She gave me a well-perfumed joy.
She told me how God made me Black and worthy.
She gave me lullabies badly but beautifully sung,
she gave me midnight snacks when I couldn't sleep.
My mother gave me love. Gave me life.
She knew, surely, what awaited me outside her door.
She knew what she and Dad could not stop,
knew the world outside of Barbies and Sesame Street
and songs and bubbles and hair barrettes
was plotting my demise, that it waited
to gulp each of my little girl giggles.
She knew it, so she filled me up to the brim
with every dream and every smile and every assurance
that I was made beautiful and full of a life
that mattered. That nothing could steal that.
She knew the world would threaten that peace,
but that those sparkling moments,
that love, that life, that beauty
were all worth fighting for.

.em In Which I Am Too Political To Read At Your School

A rose, single, silent, and soft, opens—
red petals tender, innocent, fragrant.
What beauty! How holy! Peace, unbroken
in the rose's solid stem. O, ancient
wonder, rose of unsullied joy, I sing
to the majesty of your sun-loved face—
your color so pure, petal fine as wing,
leaf's thin veins a natural puzzle of lace.
Even your thorns are worthy of my praise,
their spikes but soldiers keeping you from harm,
a stab could set my fingers all ablaze,
but still your grace would silence all alarm—

very classic straight-laced

> except the rose was black and you killed it, black and you silenced it, black
> and you raped it, black and it could not vote, black and it got in the wrong
> garden so you had to use pesticide, had to poison its water and all the
> little black rose babies, had to stop teaching it to read, it was black so you
> pulled it up by the roots with a knife shaped just like America, just like the
> government, just like whiteJesus, just like your mouth leaking bless your
> heart, you severed its roots and you chewed them whole and you smiled
> as it withered, searching for home.

then oranges, new tone

The Hymn Of The Dogwood Tree

This is only the branch of a Dogwood tree; An emblem of WHITE SUPREMACY.
A lesson once taught in the Pioneer's school, That this is a land of WHITE MAN'S RULE.
The Red Man once in an early day, Was told by the Whites to mend his way.
The negro, now, by eternal grace, Must learn to stay in the negro's place.
In the Sunny South, the Land of the Free, Let the WHITE SUPREME forever be.
Let this a warning to all negroes be, Or they'll suffer the fate of the DOGWOOD TREE.
—popular lynching postcard poem, 1908

"I thank God for slavery—if it wasn't for slavery, I might be somewhere in Africa worshipping a tree." —Kimberly Daniels, 2018

let us praise   the roots and the leaf   /   praise   the   dangling branch //

praise the   tender throat   the wailing neck //   praise //   let   us

gather at this   dogwood   altar //   praise   each   vein

and   the   blood // the blood //   jesus   call   us   home

and   whole   //   even here   we   praise //

praise   each   shaking   branch   // the sigh of the bark rubbed raw //

dark   southern   trees /   so   far   from our   faraway   home //

praise   each   dogwood   oak / the pine of the slaveship's neverending hull /

let   us   praise lord   //   this tree   holds us   up   up   up

so   Heaven's   not   too far   away /   up   / so high   they   mistake

our praise   for   cries.

All Y'all Really From Alabama

"...The straitjackets of race prejudice and discrimination do not wear only southern labels. The subtle, psychological technique of the North has approached in its ugliness and victimization of the Negro the outright terror and open brutality of the South."

—Rev. Dr. Martin Luther King Jr., *Why We Can't Wait*

this here the cradle of this here nation—everywhere
you look, roots run right back south. every vein filled
with red dirt, blood, cotton. we the dirty word you spit
out your mouth. mason dixon is an imagined line—
you can theorize it, or wish it real, but it's the same old
ghost—see-through, benign. all y'all from alabama; we
the wheel turning cotton to make the nation move. we
the scapegoat in a land built from death. no longitude or
latitude disproves the truth of founding fathers' sacred
oath:

we hold these truths like dark snuff in our jaw,
Black oppression's not happenstance; it's law.

moment of
southernness

20

Manifest Destiny

and so he learned that the land could be called a name so he called it mine.
and so he learned it could be bordered with blood and so he called it conquest.
and he learned that the land was willing to give fruit and flower and he called it profit.
and so he saw some otherfolk planting and praising and he called them enemy.
and so he saw there were armies to guard those flowering folk and he called them prey.
and so he saw the ocean, and what was it but a highway to make more borders?
and so he saw the bright and peaceful sea and he littered it with trade—
the bodies stacked next to the crops, the textiles and the rot of disease.
and so he ground hope and God into dust and called it rights.
and so he heard the wind blowing joy over its people and he sliced it up with law.
and so he kept slicing for five hundred years.
and so he built his things around him, and so his coffers never emptied,
and so he took wives and made children. and so he gave them, too, a price.
and so he saw each blade of grass and counted it as currency.
and so his blood was transfused with gold.
and so he built a wall around himself to keep his many riches in. the walls encased with bone.
even his heart, a fortress of muscle and money.

listen, now, your past and future generations:
your hoarded haul will spoil where you stand.

Excess

Two boys, pink in their manhood, lean over a balcony, full
of teeth. Below: a brown man, skin tired of holding his bones.
Work falls in shadows around his feet.
The Puget Sound is bluer than any dream or sky. The boys loom, pink.
Is it rain? A sudden shower on this otherwise idyllic afternoon, this day
which looks painted, happy little trees? The man crosses his arms.
He looks up, I look up.
We crane our necks, we keep our eyes on the sky.
Sky, where Heaven unpeels in a sluice of excess water,
where storm ferments and sizzles down. Again, a white drop.
Then laughter, the pink mouth moving in an o and then a half circle, tooth-full. No heaven
but a white boy's mouth. No storm but the giggles bubbling up into a ball of frothy spit,
the hanging loop that lingers before it drops, so close to that brown head, then the flat splat
on the cement below.
The boys slink away, pleased with their game.
The man still looks up—maybe to heaven, maybe just the clouds.

In Freeland, All The Beaches Are Owned

for A, P, & Y

Morning breaks, cool and open over our heads—
in Freeland, everything is beautiful. Houses so clean
the grass shines like soap. We can hear the water, waves lead
us ever closer. Sky a blue that makes me think we're free—
is this land our land? We, emboldened by the wind
and how it slips around our arms, blows our eyes open,
ask a woman how to make it to the beach. She is not kind.
All this is private, she says. Her dog looks unheld by his leash. Then,
the sky darkens, & I remember the color of my skin.
The way she curls her lips lets me know this is a warning:
we wouldn't want anyone to get mad, would we? What a sin,
it seems, to think my comfort is not temporary.
American flags shield the houses and their private stretch of beach.
How do those stripes trap the air so it, too, is just out of my reach?

Sharks!

Dead sharks emit a pheromone that turns off a live shark's feeding impulse and warns them of potential danger.

"For where two or three gather in my name, there am I with them." —Holy Bible, NIV

orca :: shark killer
orca :: big as a nation
orca :: they, who always shooting up the block
orca :: with a blue and red flag
orca :: who floss with shark liver
dead shark :: siren
dead shark :: gave his life so othershark may live
dead shark :: a sort of messiah
two or more gathered :: God
two sharks smelling death :: two sharks still alive, still blessed
one black person's fear :: siren
one black person running :: two black people running
two or more black people running :: we all running, so help us God
we all running :: we know it's danger close
we can smell the blood even it don't show up, red, on our hands.

Sonnet For The Man Screaming Himself Into Existence At Bellevue ER

By now, I can't speak, and even though I know I
won't die here, I can't be sure. Neon's coming up in the bucket I
balance on my thighs. By now, I can't speak, I
open my mouth and a fist comes up to punch me silent. I
am in and out of my head, my body. I
can see the other patients, see a man whose feet are seeping out in sores, I
hear him refuse the IV, refuse this diabetes diagnosis, I
see the way life dangles itself in front of him like a bowl of hard candy, I
see his eyes and their wild wild glow. The man in the next cot screams *I*
I I I I I I I
as if to say, I am a man and a man deserves life, I
am a man who had a mother, I've known more than this blood seeping from my lips, I
have smiled the same smile you did when the rain cooled off a steamy summer day, I
have these rights if that's all I have. I have more than the right to die.

Love In The Time Of Pandemic

in the universe of my parents' backyard
i stood in the grass and the wind gave greeting—
it blew on my back, the small and the large of it
like a ghost lover's hand—have all my lovers been ghosts?
and the wind blew around my neck,
trailing kisses of sweet air—a kiss to name my skin
as something loved and soft, as if created just for this—
the wind said, stand still, and it ran fingers through my hair—
my afro tied up in an african scarf and spilling over its side,
glowing black in the sunlight (which is its mother, it holds shadows
like a treasure, a moonlit gift).
the wind ran its fingers through my hair and over my arms
and through my legs and between my parted lips
and i have never known that God could hold me this completely,
could tell me, in one astounding breath
that i am loved. that i am healed and will be healed,
that healing can mean taking me out of this world and into heaven
that it can mean locking all my doors and telling me stay home
can mean the summer bringing fruit through the earth's open mouth
and time bringing forth more time and more time and more—
and i know there will be a time when the wind
does not know my name and when i'm straining to hear
the voices of my ancestors and even your voice saying hello,
but i know that will be healing, too,
that a chill always makes way for a grateful warmth.

Ainteenem

the cool salt of your Newports
the hot dark sand of them on the porch
the night mirroring the blackened ash
you my auntie but I don't really know you
don't know more than this smell, this smoke
don't know why you always smirking but not happy
auntie were you even laughing in that casket two weeks ago?
even in death, you carefree like a Newport
you toxic like one too, you, even dead, make *us* feel like disease—
auntie, I found you today in the smoke
coming out of a poet's lips
auntie, I found you there and wished you away
auntie, you wouldn't leave me be so I inhaled—
maybe, auntie, I can love you if I just breathe deep—

Hostile Environment

after Solmaz Sharif

According to slave codes, slaves were not allowed to gather without a white person present
to prevent anything masters deemed dangerous: education, revolt, joy, or religious worship.
Slaves often met in secret for church.

the morning opens, HOSTILE, soft.
this morning so beautiful, so calm it makes these fields look fertile with fruit
instead of blood, the HOSTILE thorns just glittering teeth in the distance.
we here to praise him, HOSTILE god,
here to hear the word, its holy HOSTILITY, its promise that there is more than death in death—
here, the shaky preacher's wail, HOSTILE against the walls of the shack,
this church, a gathering of worshippers, HOSTILE and gaping—
we stomp our feet, each beat burning, HOSTILE and loud,
we shouting now and Master's sure to hear.
maybe he'll let us be, HOSTILE, maybe he'll slide a hand around his wife's HOSTILE hip
and make this morning move
or maybe
the spirit of the Lord, its HOSTILE sugartongue, will draw him to the horsewhip,
HOSTILE and gentle in its quick, quiet rage—

God Made My Whole Body

and the way it moves, and the way it shakes and jiggles and plops, and God made my smile and the thousand tears that fall from my eyes, God made the sun and the moon and the leaf held loosely in my godson's perfect little hand, and God made the summer breeze and the guitar Ron Isley crooned over, and God made the grass and the bugs and the dogs and the trees, and God made all of our bodies to make waste, and God made even the waste that lives in us, and God made the way the world spins and the way it will shake us right off if we don't act right, and God made the rivers which make it possible for us to drink, and God made the clouds which hold the rain, and God made the birds which fly and the wolves that howl. God made the folds of my brain and the thoughts that burrow there. God made my belly, my uterus and all the little eggs which might become children—God made the doubt that rests there, like bubbling gas. God made the silence I wrap around myself some nights, alone. God made the music we sing and the music we hate. God made the ears which help us stay balanced, help us to hear what people say behind our backs and in front of them. God made sweet potato pie and aunties and mamas who know how to add just enough nutmeg. God made my whole body. And God made my grandma and her gold tooth, and God made my grandma and her curly wig, and God made my grandma I didn't know, and God made my grandpa who was a ghost, and my grandpa who was a terror. God made fear and the way it slices us up thin and flimsy, God made the way a hand quivers before it strikes. God made pain. God made the blood which runs and keeps us running. God made an everlasting red.

A Poem About The Body

I.

I don't know new words to say about the body,

but I know that my body is new,

changed from the bones of my youth—

at 6, my gifted resource teacher would ask *have you eaten today? I can see your ribs!*

At 14, I wished I could reclaim those ribs that stuck out of my shirt,

those knobby hips—they would have been so beautiful

poking, slightly, over the lip of a low rise jean—

so beautiful, those bones.

II.

He said, you have a woman's body but, to me, it wasn't a compliment.

What he meant: this is a body I wish the other girl had.

it is natural to compare women's bodies.

it is natural to have one girl and have one other.

it is natural to use bodies where hearts should be.

this is a body I can hold in my hands and marvel at my own

hands, their facility.

this is a body that affirms my own manhood.

He did not deserve my body.

I did not give him my body.

III.

He said a part of me was universal. That part, I'll leave for you to guess.

He said that part was big enough for the Black men and small enough for the White.

I wondered what that part could do to a man. I wondered if I really had that kind of power.

IV.

There was never any room for you in these jeans.

There will never be any room for you in these jeans.

Sometimes, there's barely room for me.

V.

I don't know new words to say about the body,

        but I know my body is new,

                changed from the bones of my youth—

I look in the mirror and wonder how I earned these curves,

look, these are the breasts of my dreams—why did I ever dream of breasts?

What does it mean to see my own body and think, *now you're finished. Now you're real.*

What of those years in a 32 cup? What of A, of B?

So strange, this alphabet—

tells us who we are and makes us spell it out, letter by letter.

VI.

Twice in my life, I've stopped eating.

At first, because I didn't have the time. Stress ate me alive.

Then, the thin wrists and flat stomach looked good.

Then, I had to impress his parents. I had to fit in the palm of his hand.

Then, I had to smile and make straight A's and volunteer this way and that way,

then, I was just discovering my body, but preferred it empty.

VII.

When I was young, I always drew all women with cleavage,

with little waists and bow legs.

How many little girls across this planet see a paper doll-body

and wish on every star, wish to the man in the moon,
wish to God and to the editors of *Cosmopolitan*—*just let me be pretty,*
let my body fill out but, Lord, not too much. Lord, give me curves but give me the right ones.
Lord, make me worthy of worship, make me beautiful.

VIII.

How many calories can I burn worrying over my waistline?

IX.

My first prom and I felt too fat to dance.
My first prom, tenth grade, no date but my sister—
the boy I loved with his pretty girl, his look-how-he-can-sling-her-hold-her-pick-her-up—
my stomach, bulging in the sequined dress I'd been so proud to buy,
the dress whose skin held tightly to my belly, reminded me that this was my load to bear.

X.

On the street, I brace myself for the eyes.
Men in their cars on their bikes on their own two feet watch me. Some shout.
Pretty lady, pretty girl, they say.
They deem me worthy of this bastardized praise.
Is this worthiness enough?

For The Men Who Made Sure I Knew They Did Not Love Me

First of all /ain't nobody want you anyway / nobody asked to smile in your face / and / hug your neck / and / ignore the brown ring around your stank collar / and / cook you meals / real meals / with grease / and a foot put in / nobody asked / to watch you eat / with your whole fat tongue / and each little piggy / spit-shined / and food all in your mouth / jostling while you talk / about nothing / about how much you love my cooking / my cooking and not me / nobody asked you / for kisses so wet I had to towel down after / for kisses so stolen I had to call the police / for kisses so sweet I almost believed them // nobody asked for too much tongue / for the trick of pleasure masquerading as love // ain't nobody asked for songs / for your off-key whining / for your on-key whining but still sour somehow / for your fingers on the piano / for your fingers on the piano while somebody else sings about you / nobody asked for love songs you did not mean / or even understand //ain't nobody asked to read your poems / your term papers / your very long emails with typos / nobody went to college twice to cross your t's / dot your i's// nobody asked to be loved by you / I know I wasn't loved by you / you ain't gotta tell me / I know the shape of unlove / it looks like your mouth / slick with joy / while your eyes / dead / flat

In Critique Of Black Female Demonization, Not Miscegenation

how many times did you practice
calling me bulldog, ugly, furious plague,
before it tasted like truth?
in the schoolyard, did you watch the little black girls
running in the sun and note how that sun
baked them darker? did you learn to spell their names
with a poisonous tongue?
in the locker room, now infamously presidential,
did you trade stories of conquests
and lie to make yours lighter,
or is my body a prize only when it's splayed open,
spread, with sweetness, for you?
did you let my body's gift curdle in your crude retelling?

does it hurt each time you call us unwantable? does your mother's face fade deeper into black?

somewhere, in a past we both know and always return to,
i watch you, beaten, in the field. watch you, clubbed to pulp by the Big Blue Badge.
there, i clean your wounds and kiss your body better,
heal you with salve and a meal cooked slow—
somewhere, i put my body between yours and harm,
between a blinding white and your black—
somewhere, i even put my body on the cross—

does this sacrifice mean nothing? don't you understand how woman i am, to bear you,
feed you, clothe you, even beat you if it means you'll grow?
don't you see the mirror you shatter when you tell me what you think I'm not?

look, my dark love, at your hands. see what they can't grasp when you let me go?

Words With Friends

I had never played before because I didn't want to connect with someone I didn't know. I played with you. And I was right. There is no one familiar on the other side of a minefield of yellow blocks, plenty of words but no meaning. I remember that afternoon you let me try on your shoe—so many sizes too big. My foot swam in it, so many dark spaces to hide. Your eyes, too. I remember when you showed me your sculptures, their gorgeous metal arms. Cold, like yours. I remember the way your braces shone in the sunlight. A puzzling sparkle. I learned to spell fear and love with the same black letters. Learned how to see you through some cliché, maybe rose-colored glasses?—or maybe just my own two eyes, finally. I learned that unrequited is an easy word to chew—it falls right off the bone, tender barbecue. I learned that you could play many games, simultaneously. Your hand on this board and that one and that one way across the USA—I learned that my heart is a wooden chiclet block, whittled away by fingertips holding, holding, then deciding it just won't fit. I remember you always spelled words that you couldn't use in a sentence, that were only useful for the points. I think about all those unusable words. The games you won saying things you couldn't even understand. I think about the shape of your tongue. How strange it must feel for it to sit, split in your two-sided mouth. How the compass of it, north & south, maps its way through my heart and right back out.

Bestiary Of Bad Kisses

The Frog

It isn't the summer day
or the slight breeze swishing
my hair across my neck
that I remember.
Just the tongue sliding, sticky, up my cheek—
> how it, days before, had slipped between my teeth
> in the abandoned art studio on campus, how I'd shut my eyes
> against it, how I'd pretended this wasn't just a slimy mistake—
just the way I knew, after that tongue,
unasked for and unwanted, marked my face with spit—
this would be the last time I let a boy kiss me,
knowing I did not want him.

The Anteater

I am not an anteater expert. I don't know if they really suck up ants like a vacuum,
but that's what they taught me in school, so that's what I believe. What they didn't
teach me was how it feels to be sucked dry, to be a mound of brown ants at the nose
of an anteater, to be kissed so hard it makes a *pop* against my neck, to be tugged sore,
to carry a purple hickey like a flashing siren, blaring *owned, owned, owned*! What did
this boy think was buried beneath my skin? Were you a fleshy prospector, mining
for the light tucked just under these white rocks, my clean, young bones?

The Bulldog

swearing I like it   swearing that all women like it   you coat my lips   in slobber
and smile.   even in the morning   with a sleep-coated tongue   with sour
breath   sour   teeth   sour   slobber   sour sour—
you close your mouth over mine   start your steady grumble   like it's that good already.
I try to remember   how charming I find your wrinkled thinking brow   your sweet voice
under this kiss.   I try to remember   that I think this could be love   but even thinking
is hard to do   in this kiss I can't escape.   even if I initiate   you find a way
to make it yours   to drown me in your leaking tongue.   you remind me how free
it feels   to breathe.

Love Note: Surely

with first line from Gwendolyn Brooks

Surely you stay my certain own, you stay
obtuse. Surely your kisses were little poisons
gripping tight my lips, my arms, mapping their way
across my unsure body. Surely, this fission

is a gift—a gilded parcel laced like God, scent
of Mother Mary's milkbreath and her virgin promise,
that virginal mirror, me. Surely, I was sent—
and, incidentally, that other *she*, to put you on notice—

hearts aren't toys for juggling, no, the blood
too sticky to really ever disappear—
surely you know that. Surely, your own beating brick withstood
the blows I tried to strike with my unrelenting care.

The morning opens, now, without your sun-blacked face—
the bluejays and morningbirds sing away your waste.

It Is Entirely Possible For A Black Girl To Be Loved

see me,   Black as I am   and call me beautiful   no revolution necessary,

no brave needed, just loving me   it is not unusual to love me,   Black as I am

it is not because I'm so strong   so exotic   so 'walk on the wild side'   what side?

see my skin   it's not chocolate   or coffee   or caramel   it is inedible

it is nothing to see with colonizer's eyes   nothing to trap   with pity   or praise

nothing to bruise, to make purple with your power   my skin is soft like anything soft

it is a reflection of God   it is a heavenly mirror   don't you see that? you're there, too—

Black as I am, I can shine anything back   even the sun   wants to cling to me.

Summer Vacation In The Subjunctive

If I were a woman. If I were a wanted woman. If I were a woman with soft fingers. If I were on a beach with a man—if he was a man, if a man can be a man before he acts like a man. If I were on a beach with a man and he held my hand. If I liked my hand being held, even if it was held at the wrong angle. If my wrist was wringing in pain but I kept it there. If my heart were held wrong, like my hand. If I kept it there. If I was kept. If I was kept in pain. If I were pain. If I were a woman—if I were a woman before I was a woman. If I were a woman who knew her body like a woman knows her body. If a woman knew. If I knew. If I were on a beach with that man—if, this time, that man dissolved into sand. If the sand became hot under my feet but my feet were gold. If a woman were made of sun. If I were made of sun. If I burned the world around me until it shone beautiful and brown. If this burning was called healing. If the healing made light.

Contrapuntal With Gladys Knight And Infidelity

oh yes   I am afraid to love you,

I heard you,   a man who smiles

with your top teeth only   hiding something at the bottom.

Oh yes   I heard, love

the whole grapevine   can fit under the molars

can hide under a tongue,   even as it says *love, love, you*

it can grow, love   through my ears and down my throat, love,

it can speak to me in my sleep—   even as you hold me, love,

my eyes are grape leaves, love,   covering the most bitter fruit.

even the birds sing this sour song.   I bet you're wondering how I knew—

You could have told me yourself.   I wonder, too—

Am I worthy of love?   I am

oh yes I am   the grapevine

The Self Returns, A Year Later

When I wept to him, I didn't know my soul was slipping from between my teeth, floating out to look at me. *Girl*, it said. *Who are you?* I didn't know. I didn't recognize my own voice as it sat in the air between us. His eyes looked strange. They were the same eyes he'd worn when I met him. His hands were a stranger's hands—weren't they the ones that held me, that painted a world of dreams we both knew could dissolve with just a little soap and water? I said, *why are you doing this to me?* What I meant: *why did I do this to myself?* His apology carried the same stench as every other word he spoke. What kisses could he give with a mouth like that? Greedy kisses. But I wanted to give. And I gave until someone said *enough*. God blew my eyes open, as if shooing dust off a table, as if swishing sand off the inside of my arm. It burned but I was so glad to see the world again, to see the golden ropes which held me here, to God, to my family, to this world which wanted me, after all. When I wept I wondered, *what is love? Not this.* I wept—a new kind of death—I put out my hand and heard my pretty blue soul calling my name. It looked from him to me, and what I want to tell you is what my soul saw:

nothing and nothing and no one and nothing and not a single warm familiar thing.

Aubade With Lalah Hathaway And Rachelle Ferrell

I'm coming back / just to give you my love /there's a part of me that lives in you
—Lalah Hathaway and Rachelle Ferrell, "I'm Coming Back,"

—but what the song doesn't say is that there's a part of you that lives in me—there's a piece of you still flowering, still sucking on the soil in my heart—there, something still grows, however weakly—there, I imagine that you and I still amble toward love or something like it—somewhere, we're waking up together like the aubades that seem so untrue—there, we still live in the walls of this song, where coming back is beautiful and not regressive, where coming back means a natural return and not a backpedal—somewhere is not here—here is not love—love is not you—what the song doesn't say is that part of me that lives in you can still breathe its way back to me—it can, carrying your scent, your sweet sweet—it can come back to me and show me what seedlings were there—there is a flower, still, even if the soil was not rich enough to grow—there is a flower even within the seed—

Aubade: My Mother Calls Home

An *mhm* is softer, sweeter than yes—
out of my mother's mouth, it's a song—how
beautiful, this flavor of English, best
served over the phone, best from mother, now
miles and miles away from home, Greensboro
and its clay, its quiet constellation
of field flowers, the unrelenting glow
of porch lamps—lemons filled with light—the sun
is a dull bulb in comparison. Today,
I wake to my mother's voice, her sister
on the other side of the line—there's a
comfort in knowing this language can stir
the air until it feels like a mother's
tongue: comfortable enough to drop some r's.

Sonnet with Kanye West and Late Uncle

"Don't rush to get grown, drive slow, homie." —Kanye West, "Drive Slow"

Back then, it was as simple as forever—
moms and dads did not die and Kanye West
was who we listened to every day without guilt. Summer
was endless and full of cartoons and the sweet wet
scent of cereal milk in the morning. I remember that day,
all the cousins crammed in Junior's room, listening,
almost holding our breaths in the dark of that Hale County
house. *Graduation Day* played quietly. There'd be no disturbing
the adults who cackled down the hall, strong and invincible.
Back then, all I wanted was to be cool enough to know the lyrics—
not the chorus, but the obscure ones. It was simple,
then, the way we swore July would never end. Too young to fear it,
we let death, or worse, time, creep up behind us—
the song bounced on and hid the darker notes: tragedy, loss.

Greatest Nigger Who Ever Lived

in the selfie he is currently texting to "Lula Mae,"
the man next to me on flight 4853
to Columbia, dressed in a black turtleneck
and a thick double chain,
smirks at the camera an arm's length from his face,
below which, the blue bubble (his words)
proclaims him "The Greatest Nigger Who Ever Lived."
Perhaps I should be looking out the window and not at his phone,
but our thighs are touching
because the armrest that should prevent such intimacy is up,
and I think of his heavy, soft chuckle when he struggled out
of his seat to let me in (a chuckle brown as any uncle—

       and maybe
       I think all older black people
       are my family,
       and I did have an aunt named Lula Mae
       who I did not know well,
       but I knew her laugh out of any laugh
       in the whole smiling world
       because it was an incomparable shrill,
       the greatest, maybe,
       somewhere, glass is breaking even at its ghost—),
and maybe when I'm older I will marry
a Great Nigger—not the greatest; that position's taken—
and he will keep a picture of me on his cell phone
just like The Greatest does of Lula Mae
when she was decades younger but just as fine,
smiling, with the most glittering hint of mischief in her dimple,

the soft focus of the camera incapable of hiding
the way Lula's big white teeth
make everything greater greater greater greater greater—

Reparations Now, Reparations Tomorrow, Reparations Forever

using text from George Wallace's 1963 Inaugural Address

I.

The Governor Speaks

before I begin—

        patience.

my heart, by which I mean my anxious country,

        will never forget the folks we beat:

                the little lady who couldn't see too well,

                the blessed opposition,

                the vote—

this debt, this duty to every man, woman, and child:

        no Black shall have his livelihood, his future.

        we have stolen it away

        with our happy money,

        Jefferson Davis' loving blood—

II.
Mo'   Money   Interlude

money got   mo' problems   money got a maserati   money got mo' money

money got ya mama   and ya daddy too   money got no expiration date

money got pennies and papercuts   money got a white man on its face   money got faces

money is nothing black   even the ink is green   money don't know your name

money paid the price   for our sins? for our freedom?   money got math we can't learn

money says it trusts in God   what God trusts money?   Jesus, Money, and Joseph

money, descended from Ham   money watches us, naked   money curses us, rich & poor

money said *separate but equal*   money said *3/5ths a man*   money said *four score and seven years ago*

III.

Altar Call – The Poet Reproduces Wallace's Exact Words

IN THE NAME OF THE GREATEST PEOPLE THAT HAVE EVER TROD THIS EARTH, I DRAW THE LINE IN THE DUST AND TOSS THE GAUNTLET BEFORE THE FEET OF TYRANNY AND I SAY: SEGREGATION NOW, SEGREGATION TOMORROW, SEGREGATION FOREVER.

IV.

Praise Break: The Governor Channels The Spirit of His god

Riot!
    Children, you can write that down.
        Mississippi was a B-29 bomber in this war to stop residential integration.
Hypocrisy!
      Let us send this message:
          we, tyranny, shall put our heel on the neck of Washington,
           of those insipid judges who send smoke signals to the White House,
              those who are not worth the honor of their race.
Hear me, Southerners!
        Your hearts live in the soil of Dixeland.
        Your rock-ribbed patriotism, your flaming spirit
        for segregation and freedom
        has
          been
            blessed
              by
                God!

Alabama is the center of the world.

God has given this to us—a heritage of unimpeachable authority and power.
This ungodly government, these degenerates are the very opposite of Christ.

Children, say a prayer for our dollars, our founding fathers, our faith, our power.

wants more than a passive action
something continuous, that ppl are working on

V.
A Case for Reparations

When, Governor, can we enjoy the full richness of the Great American Dream?
My grandmother was a sharecropper. My grandfather beat his Black wife and
Black children. My uncle was arrested for a crime he didn't commit—in America,
even the shadows of Black people are black enough to hide all innocence. Some
nights, I dream of being killed like Emmett Till or Trayvon Martin or Sandra
Bland or [INSERT BLACK PERSON'S NAME HERE]. Some nights, I insert
my name there. Is that the American Dream? Governor, President, Mayor, Boss
Man, Woman With A Cell Phone or a Police Badge or a Bank Account and The
Skin Tender Enough To Make Murder Legal, when will you be tired of the taste
of Black blood? Sometimes, I'm singing a song and you make that feel like death.
Sometimes, I'm dancing a dance and you make that feel like shame. Sometimes,
I'm sitting on my porch just trying to eat a damn melon and you make that feel
like I'm selling my Black soul. My parents told me I could be anything, even God.
That's the least I'm owed—to know I'm worth heaven, yes, but also worth a life on
earth. My mother told us we were pretty enough to be dolls, pretty enough to be
praised in the Book of Barbie. That's the least I'm owed—a face, skin, hair so obvi-
ously, inherently, objectively beautiful it's frozen in plastic and sold to kids all over
America to hug and love and look at with the eyes of *dreams.* What, you think all
I want is money? What, you think *money* can ever repay what you stole? Give me
land, give me all the blood you ripped out of our backs, our veins. Give me every
snapped neck and the noose you wove to hoist the body up. Give me the screams
you silenced in so many dark and lustful rooms. Give me the songs you said were
yours but you know came out of our lips first. Give me back Martin Luther King,
Jr. and Malcolm X and Medgar Evers. Give me back the beauty of my hair. The
swell of my hips. The big of my lips. Give me back the whole Atlantic Ocean. Give
me a never-ending blue. And a mule.

read that fights safely

doesn't want reparations w/o meaning

after civil war promise of land, but never given, claiming it

I Find The Earring That Broke Loose From My Ear The Night A White Woman Told Me The World Would Always Save Her

I remember:

that earring made me feel so free, so full of beauty—the kind that you might notice. Beauty that could make my shoulders glow. I remember her face, alight with a devious curiosity in the porchlight of the house party—that party in that city which slathered a film over its racism with clean streets and yard signs proclaiming inclusion. That city in that American state which legally excluded Black residents in 1844, which entered the union, big, proud, and white. Does it matter that this woman was not evil, did not send bombs to kill children in a far-off country, did not buy or sell a single slave? Picking up the earring, unwearable until I find another hook on which to hang it from my ear, I remember, again, the words and their cool sting. *I'm a white woman, people protect us.* Does it matter what I said to invite these words? Does it matter that I did not invite these words? Does it matter that she thought this was a joke, a sign that she was on the "right side," a way to pass a moment under the porchlight? I've been thinking about intention lately, how I'm always asked to consider how good a person is, what they meant versus what they said. I think about the man who called me colored at a hotel in 2019. I think about the n-word out of a white person's mouth. About erasure. I wonder about the road to hell, which, they say, is paved in these same intentions—good. George Zimmerman intended to protect his sidewalk from Trayvon's body, invasively alive. George Washington intended to protect America from Britain's oppression—nevermind those oppressed Black bodies. Yes, I am weaving a rope between George Zimmerman and George Washington. Yes, I am saying it. My country tis of thee, sweet land of white supremacy. When she said it, my face could barely twist into anything but fatigue. I am tired over and over again of being told I am not human enough to matter. The white poet rages against me on Facebook. Maybe he imagines my blood against his ivory tower. Maybe he imagines the many bricks my foremothers and fathers built—LucillePhyllisGwendolynPaulLawrenceLangstonSoniaMayaNikki—

tumbling at the flick of his well-educated thumb. Is even my degree a different color, relegated to the back of a bus, a book? The business of poetry so thick with privilege, so smothered in the rust of its old gates—how can you breathe among all that rot? On the news, the man they call president tells us to go back from where we came. I think of all the lost ones thrown over boats, the ones locked away in cages, the ones here, sitting as American as the day is long and still called wrong. The earring says *I once was lost* when I find it, tells me it can be repaired. It is an earring of the struggle. It wants that ear it once called home, it wants to touch my brown skin and reflect it in its orbiting gold. I look for my pliers, my jewelry kit. The work is always the thing that makes us whole again.

I Cannot Talk About The South Without Talking About Black Women

a golden shovel after Lucille Clifton

My grandmothers made America,
                    made
            the fibers that made us
warm, made us invincible—heroines.

To tell you who they are, I must start with who they are not:
        servants, kitchen-bound mammies, silently obedient wives—

                                        we
            can't, in our modern comforts, imagine the survival they learned
                    was theirs to claim, can't hold the
            the light they burned through this colonial darkness, what tricks
            this nation, this American South pulled, minute by minute, to

                                        keep
                            my grandmothers convinced: the
                body you're in is not enough, your race
                and your gender work together
                to mark you *less*, to mark you *takeable*, but
                what they didn't know was that my grandmothers still had
                an unmovable strength, enough to
                build a bridge from here to Heaven. I know when I leave
                this broken earth I'll find them there, sweetening every hour.

My grandmothers raised a generation of American men.
There is no other way to
                    say this. Look at any Southern family and you'll find,
somewhere, in a past most will not claim, a Black woman. These men who call themselves
bootstrapping and self-made, somewhere there's a Black woman and
her unthanked hands who lifted them to where they are now.

My father tells a story of the sons of his grandmother's employers. How they,
instead of the pension she was promised, decided to give her a damned
old tire. An old suitcase, dusty in the yard. What
thanks is this for the years she raised that family, for the care they

cannot

forget? My father could never forgive

those men, their Southern tradition. Their American tradition. Even

now, they tell us Black women are going to save this whole
nation with votes or magic or our style taken and renamed. But this is no longer the land of massas
and mammies, and we are only superheroines for our own daughters and sons—

my grandmothers did not give their lives

for me to keep nursing this country, to keep shucking and jiving in

a

bizarro American Dream—

my grandmothers are worth more than this corrupt remembering.
Now, there is no room for the

Dixieland lie:

we

no longer hold these truths you made
us accept. Under God, yes. We hear Him
singing a song of powerful love
despite the United Hate of America.

Grandmothers, women made
of salt and spirit, you are faith, continuous. Continue us—
raise us to be heroes and heroines,
to tell this country that we are not
mules, not beasts. You, an army of workers and wives—

                                                    we
                                                        hid
                                              our
                    fears and woes in your indestructible, ever-present ladyness—
the blood you passed down to us is all we will ever need to
                                                        save
                                                        our
                                                        lives.

Friendly Skies, Or, Black Woman Speaks Herself Into God

—we're taxiing at an airport named after american president ronald reagan. people tell me he was an american hero. sometimes, labels are jumbled in the big dark bag we call manifest destiny. sometimes, things get lost in its velvet mouth.

—as we move across the land in a machine built for sky, we wait for the flight attendant to tell us how to be safe, how to will ourselves alive thirty thousand feet in the air if we find ourselves falling to an inevitable end. how to build a raft from breath alone to face a gulping sea.

—our attendant, Valerie, is Black. her braids hang, a holy rope, in a high ponytail. her eyes, divinely familiar. when the disembodied voice booms over the plane speakers, we see her mouth moving in time with its words. *to ensure your safety*, she says. *secure your mask before helping others.* her lips make the shape of our salvation.

—reader, this might be how you felt sitting in the movie theater's strobe-lit box when you saw *Black Panther*, when you realized a Black person could feel as big as God, could save the world and make it home in time for dinner, run a whole country against no white background, could know all the land and its secrets *and* roam the afterworld, leisurely resting after a life of nothing colonized, after all the sweat of work done just for self, of work unstolen and unenslaved.

—and i know Valerie isn't God but i also know that she is, standing here, commanding this voice we thought was faceless, using her earthly body to show us the way. here, with her hands which will pour us fizzy drinks in our little plastic cups, usher trash from our laps into an unknown abyss—i know if this thing goes down in a fiery cocoon, she will part every sea to cradle us, she will speak to us through the fire—*you are that you are.*

An Experiential And Intellectual Discourse On The N-Word

the first time you called me nigger

       you said, *you can't play with us.*

the second time you called me nigger,

       I was too smart. too many books for a black black brain.

the third time, nigger

       was painted thickly on your picket fence,

       was gray as a house on the wrong side of the tracks,

       was laced in a bag of crack and woven, tenderly,

niggerniggernigger

       on the pages of the case files,

       in the orange of the last suit I ever wore.

       times four through ten,

nigger get back

       at the ballot box, in the Oval Office,

       in the hair gel and starchcollar of our American President.

eleven niggernuggets

       shoved down my throat

       and the throats of my babies—

       even our arteries know this name,

       know the Golden Arches and their

niggerbop.

only good nigger is a dead nigger,

       you said, when you shot me still at twelve years old.

the thirteenth time, you painted your face in

nigger

and wore it for Halloween.
the fourteenth time you called me nigger,

you said pretty for a black—

then, just black.

by the hundredth time, you didn't have to say the word at all—

n and *i* and *g* and *g* and *e* dripping on your tongue, *r* clinging
like rot to your dog teeth.

Superman's Girlfriend Lois Lane No. 106

using words from the comic book

on this daily planet, my life is good luck, all supermen at my service—I should get the pulitzer prize on the backs of metropolis' black community / wait / tenements perplex me—how can I break through this plague, their suspicious speech, these slick-mouthed babies and their knock-slam slang // homeless ghosts on this daily planet, what is the reason for their weary report / look how the sun shines sweet and pretty on their rat-infested slums // it's okay, I'm right / I'm whitey, never forget // Little Africa is dejected, a neighborhood of frustration / I'll step into this machine and transform, a startling switch / Black for a day only / the hum zoom of the world staring / the smoke of white fragility / its gloomy firetrap // Black is beautiful / have you met it before, reporter / the eternal struggle of life against death by darkness / a life of *please*, look me straight in the eye / the constant confrontation of being Black and alive in a white man's world / a universal outsider // so alien, even Superman couldn't risk loving you//

Redlining

Oh, what? You thought I didn't belong here?
You thought your street was me-proof? Thought here
was a place only lilies could grow? Can you hear
my skin before you see it? Can you hear
the rap I'm blasting down your perfect street? Here,
take it—every beat will fight for me. If you can hear
it, that means I'm winning, that means you can't hurt me here.
Means I'm belonging if it's the last thing I do. Did you hear
the one about the black girl who just wanted to mind her
own business in a country, state, city, suburb where
their only business is making sure I'm not here?
Where my face my body my God my hair
even my right to write this sonnet right here
is policed, is stared down, is burned fast as ether.

Oil Change

When the mechanic asks me how I'm doing,
I can see the way his teeth shine a rotting white,
the way a smile glistens before it gobbles—
his eyes linger—over my face, and I don't look to see
if he's looking at my thighs, the brown curve of them,
their only desire to be cool in the Alabama heat.
I pull in, and this is when the cage starts building itself around me—
I cannot escape when I'm over the bay,
when the man below is screwing and unscrewing the pieces of my car,
its hood an open, helpless mouth.
Before, the mechanic asked me, for far too long,
what I'm doing on this side of town.
The sticker from my previous oil change read "not here."
I think of the safety of "not here," the brown of it.
I wonder if it's my skin he questions,
but then, those teeth again, his eyes shrinking
behind his gaping mess of lips—the silence
he fills with that grin, the way he cocks his head just so—
and now I'm breathing faster, the walls of the garage stand, stagnant,
mocking—what would happen, I wonder,
if I simply turned the ignition and sped away?
Would these men explode, would I explode, too?
Surely, heaven is a place where men can't make anyplace
a dangerous corner—
surely, there, a smile is a smile and not a taunt.
Maybe, there, when I look over to see the mechanic,
draped through my window, hand hanging so loose it could drop

into my lap, maybe there, instead of the smile,
his pink face would dissolve into a thousand butterflies,
searching for sugar
instead of skin.

Catalog Of Things In Which There Is Still God

Alabama in the summer.
> or winter
> or autumn
> or spring.

The crescent-shaped growl
> scratching, moving
>> out
>> of Celia's throat
>> or Aretha's
>> or Patti's
>> or Mahalia's—

My mother's house.

The sunlight speckling
the soapy dishwater,
the warm pull of it—
grease separating from ceramic—
> This, a line break
>> holding hostage
> my breath, the whole entire world.

My father's hands
> fixing everything, always.
Even this strange puddle of mud
we call home—this country,
a pot not finished spinning on the wheel,
this, a stolen, festering crumb—

> —you—

How To Let Go, Or, I Smudged Lost Loves Away Into The Ocean

For Y, P, A, L, M, & V

and the ocean said *give it to me* and I did, and I watched it floating out among the cross-

hatched ripples, and I prayed it away, prayed it drowned in the ever-loving ocean, and

the ocean said breathe and I did, and I let another fly from my hands to the ocean's

hand, I watched that hand pull itself toward the moon, I heard the ocean sigh and I

knew that was my own heart sighing, I knew it was my own heart unshouldering this

burden/this love, and the ocean said anything else and I said yes, and I pulled another

from my bundle and I saw his face this time when I threw him away, and the ocean

caught him on her tongue and let him dissolve there, slowly, the last thing I saw was his

smile/his greatest lie, and the ocean pulled her tongue away from shore and swallowed,

and the ocean showed me her teeth, and I understood: anything that hurts, she said, my

smile is sharper, my belly has a room shaped just like your wounds, you'll be surprised,

my darling, at how well each hurt can fit, at the way that even my killings are clean.

Acknowledgements

Many thanks to the journals and anthologies in which these poems appear or are forthcoming:

Backbone Press: "The Kid Next To Me At The 7pm Showing Of The Avengers Has A Toy Gun"
Bomb Cyclone: "What Lives In The If In Al Green's "Simply Beautiful"; "Aubade With Lalah Hathaway And Rachelle Ferrell"
Cherry Tree: "For The Men Who Made Sure I Knew They Did Not Love Me"; "Oil Change"
Ecotone: "Aubade: My Mother Calls Home"
The Evansville Review: "In Freeland, All The Beaches Are Owned"
Exit 7: "Meteor Shower"
Gravy: "Photosynthesis"
Honey Literary : "It is Entirely Possible for a Black Girl to be Loved"
Hoxie George Review: "In My Dream, I'm Shot Again and Again"; "The Self Returns, A Year Later"; "Words With Friends"
The Mississippi Review: "Sharks!"
The Missouri Review: "Contrapuntal With Gladys Knight And Infidelity"
The Offing: "Poem In Which I Am Too Political To Read At Your School"; "Sonnet For The Man Screaming Himself Into Existence At Bellevue ER"
Origins Journal: "Hostile Environment"
Paris Lit Up: "Soul Power/James Brown Time Loop"
Poem-a-Day by *the Academy of American Poets:* "All Y'all Really From Alabama"
POETRY: "Hymn of Our Jesus and the Holy Tow Truck"; "Friendly Skies, or, Black Woman Speaks Herself Into God"
Pidgeonholes: "Sonnet With Kanye West And Late Uncle"
Redivider: "Home Security"
The Rumpus: "God Made My Whole Body"; "An Intellectual and Experiential Discourse on the N-Word"; "In Critique Of Black Female Demonization, Not Miscegenation"

Shenandoah: "Reparations Now, Reparations Tomorrow, Reparations Forever"*;* "I Find
The Earring That Came Loose From My Ear The Night A White Woman Told Me
The World Would Always Save Her."
Scoundrel Time: "Mary, Don't You Weep, Or, Mary Turner Resurrected"; "Stephon Don't
You Moan, Or, To Serve And Protect"; "Hymn Of The Dogwood Tree"
South Florida Poetry Journal: "Catalog Of Things In Which There Is Still God"
Southern Humanities Review: "A Poem About The Body"; "Bestiary Of Bad Kisses"
Southern Indiana Review: "Ainteenem"; "How to Let Go, Or, I Smudged Lost Loves Away
In the Ocean"
Steel Toe Review: "Superman's Girlfriend Lois Lane No. 106"; "Redlining"
SWWIM Every day: "Summer Vacation In The Subjunctive"
The Virginia Quarterly Review: "Excess"; "Love Note: Surely"

HUB CITY PRESS

PUBLISHING
New & Extraordinary
VOICES FROM THE
AMERICAN SOUTH

Founded in Spartanburg, South Carolina in 1995, Hub City Press has emerged as the South's premier independent literary press. Focused on finding and spotlighting extraordinary new and unsung writers from the American South, our curated list champions diverse authors and books that don't fit into the commercial publishing landscape. The press has published over one-hundred high-caliber literary works, including novels, short stories, poetry, memoir, and books emphasizing the region's culture and history. Hub City is interested in books with a strong sense of place and is committed to introducing a roster of lesser-heard Southern voices.

RECENT HUB CITY PRESS POETRY

Cleave • Tiana Nobile

Mustard, Milk, and Gin • Megan Denton Ray

Dusk & Dust • Esteban Rodriguez

Rodeo in Reverse • Lindsey Alexander

Eureka Mill - 20th Anniversary Edition • Ron Rash

Magic City Gospel • Ashley M. Jones

Wedding Pulls • J.K. Daniels

Punch • Ray McManus

Pantry • Lilah Hegnauer